D1598073

WOMEN OF SCIENCE

PEGGY WHITSON

Nicole K. Orr

PURPLE TOAD
PUBLISHING

Printing   1   2   3   4   5   6   7   8   9

PUBLISHER'S NOTE: The first-person narrative in chapter one of this book is a work of fiction based on the author's research.

Jane Goodall
Katherine Johnson
Mae Jemison
Marie Curie
Peggy Whitson
Rachel Carson

Library of Congress Cataloging-in-Publication Data
Orr, Nicole K.
  Peggy Whitson / Written by: Nicole K. Orr
    p. cm.
Includes bibliographic references, glossary, and index.
ISBN 9781624694844
1. Whitson, Peggy A., 1960- — Juvenile literature. 2. Women—Astronauts—Juvenile literature. 3. Women Scientists—Juvenile literature. 4. Women—Biography— Juvenile literature. I. Series: Wonder Women/Women of Science.

 TL789. 85. A1 O77 2019
 629.45

Library of Congress Control Number: 2019949433

eBook ISBN: 9781624694837

ABOUT THE AUTHOR: Nicole K. Orr has been writing for as long as she's known how to hold a pen. She is the author of several other books by Purple Toad Publishing and she has won National Novel Writing Month eleven times. Orr lives in Portland, Oregon.

CONTENTS

Peggy Whitson's (left) life was changed forever when she watched *Apollo 11* Lunar Module pilot, American engineer, and astronaut Edwin Eugene "Buzz" Aldrin, Jr. become the second person to set foot on the moon on July 20, 1969.

Ignore the Naysayers

I was so busy on the International Space Station (ISS), there wasn't a lot of time for relaxing or hobbies. Even if I had time off, I would often find something job-related to do or an experiment to research. Bringing more work on myself often inspired NASA to give more work to the rest of my crew. I got such a reputation for this, the extra work hours came to be called "Peggy Time."

One day aboard the ISS, I picked up pen and paper. I wrote a letter, not to anyone back on Earth, but to my nine-year-old self. Maybe I did it to feel closer to home. Maybe I did it because of all the records NASA said I was breaking. I only knew that I wanted to tell my younger self her dream had come true.[1]

"Dear Younger Me," I wrote at the top of the lined notebook. "You just watched on TV as Neil Armstrong and Buzz Aldrin took the first steps on the moon." Even as I wrote the words, I felt the excitement in my stomach again. My sister and I were in bed when our parents came to get us for this important moment. It had been confusing, then thrilling. As we watched the event on TV, I felt so small, but also inspired.[2]

"Next year your dad will get his private pilot's license," I wrote. "You will get your very first ride in an airplane. The exhilarating view of the cornfields from above will inspire you to fly as well. However, it will take several years of raising and selling chickens to earn enough money to take your own flying lessons." If I closed my eyes, I could almost hear the *cluck, cluck, cluck* of the chickens. All during high school, I tended and sold them, while dreaming of flying my own plane.[3]

I turned sideways and looked through the nearest window at Earth below. I had graduated from high school the same year that NASA chose its first female astronauts. While I'd been down there, taking classes and turning in tests, women had been training to come up here to do this. I'd dreamed of doing the same, but as a kid, it had seemed impossible.

"Know that what you dream for might seem impossible, but you will be successful . . . ," I continued writing. "So ignore the naysayers, ignore the people who say you can't become an astronaut. Instead use it as motivation."[4]

NASA/NOAA Geostationary Operational Environmental Satellite (GOES) captures a view of the moon peeking over Earth's shoulder.

Peggy Whitson, wearing a thermal undergarment, prepares for a spacewalk in the Pirs docking compartment of the International Space Station. Astronauts wear many layers to protect themselves from the deadly cold of space.

That motivation had been so hard to hold on to! It had taken ten years of applying to NASA before I was accepted. Everywhere I'd turned, there had been rejection or disapproval. I could only wish my disappointed younger self had known what was coming.

I added to the letter, "All those years of anticipation will be surpassed when the solid rocket boosters ignite and you will literally roar into space." It was easy to remember that first flight back in 2002. Everything had felt new and exciting and exactly as I had imagined it to be. Back then, I'd wanted to somehow capture the experience so I could return to it later. Unfortunately, there had been just too much to do. Now, I could capture some of that wonder in my letter.[5]

Flight Engineer Peggy Whitson grows soybean plants as an experiment on the International Space Station.

"Believe it or not, you will spend more time in space than any other American astronaut and earn the nickname Space Ninja. You will grow soybeans in orbit while your father will grow soybeans on Earth. . . . You will walk, in space, 10 times! You will find that living in space can actually become a home, in spite of tools floating away."[6]

Even now, I could feel that first thrill of spaceflight shoot through me. Space had proven to be even more amazing than I'd ever imagined. It had been worth every rejection and disappointment.

"You will learn that you are so much more capable than you might imagine or dream." I signed off, "The Older You," and then looked back out the window at the glory of space.[7]

Note to Self

Though Peggy Whitson started writing a letter to her younger self while she was in space, she didn't finish it until she was back on Earth. Her letter became available to the world when it was incorporated into *CBS This Morning*'s book *Note to Self*. The idea was that, through letters written by stars to their younger selves, the book could inspire the young people of today. One of the letters was Peggy Whitson's. Other people who contributed to the 2018 book include former First Lady Michelle Obama, actor and activist Jane Fonda, comedian Russell Brand, and even Kermit the Frog.[8]

Launched into orbit on Russia's Soyuz MS-03 spacecraft, Peggy Whitson became the oldest woman to fly into space at age 56.

Green fields beneath a blue umbrella and fluffy white clouds, a granary, a colony of red barns and outbuildings, all stir memories of growing up in Iowa.

CHAPTER 2

The Farm Girl Goes to NASA

Peggy Annette Whitson was born in Mount Ayr, Iowa, on February 9, 1960. Her parents were Keith and Beth Whitson. Her sister was Kathy Bretz. The family owned a farm on the edge of Beaconsfield. As Peggy would later say in an interview, "I saw more hogs growing up than I saw people."[1]

In 1969, Peggy enrolled at Mount Ayr Community High School. It was this same year that Neil Armstrong and Buzz Aldrin landed on the moon. Their achievement inspired Peggy to become an astronaut.

In 1970, Peggy's father Keith got his pilot's license and took Peggy for a ride. It was a life-changing moment for her. She'd already known she wanted to be an astronaut, but now she wanted to fly planes, too. According to a video interview, Peggy told her sister Kathy that she wanted to be a pilot, "and my sister said, 'You can't be an airline pilot. You can only be the flight attendant.' My mom said no, that's not true. You can be whatever you want."[2]

Both of Peggy's parents played a vital role in Peggy's life. Keith showed Peggy a love for the skies, and Beth Whitson reminded her to

American physicist and astronaut Sally Kristen Ride became the first American woman in space in 1983. She followed USSR female cosmonauts Valentina Tereshkova and Svetlana Savitskaya.

never give up, not even when others tried to discourage her. "I think my parents are probably the hardest-working people I've ever met," she said. "I think I got a double dose of the dedication and stubbornness gene from them which contribute to my success."[3] Peggy's sister recognized that dedication and stubbornness. She said of Peggy, "She has a personality of someone who has a goal in mind and goes for it. And she will work her tail off to get there."[4]

In 1978, Peggy graduated from high school and enrolled at Iowa Wesleyan College. There, professors tried to persuade her to abandon her dream of being an astronaut and switch to medical school. Peggy knew Sally Ride had been chosen as NASA's first female astronaut. If Sally Ride could do it, why not Peggy Whitson? In a moment of doubt, Peggy had a meeting with James Van Allen, a well-known physicist at the University of Iowa. When she told him about her dream of becoming an astronaut, he told her manned spaceflight would soon go extinct. Spaceflight would be handled entirely by robots.[5]

NASA's Johnson Space Center in Houston is the hub of American spaceflight activity. It serves as home to the nation's astronaut corps, ISS mission operations, the Orion program, and future space enterprises.

Frustrated by the answer, Peggy pushed on anyway and, in 1981, graduated with a bachelor's degree in science. Along the way, she received numerous awards and recognitions. From 1978 to 1981, she was on the President's Honor Roll. In 1979, she was declared the State of Iowa Scholar, and in 1980, she received the Orange van Calhoun Scholarship.

The year she graduated from Iowa Wesleyan College, Peggy began attending Rice University in Houston. There, she obtained her Ph.D. in biochemistry and met her future husband, Clarence Sams. Sams was also a biochemist. The two were married on May 6, 1989.

After her years of traditional education, Whitson was ready to pursue the work of becoming an astronaut. In 1986, she began

The Blue Planet provides a backdrop for Russian Space Station Mir, after undocking from the ISS, in a photo snapped from space shuttle *Atlantis* on the 4th of July, 1995.

working at NASA's Johnson Space Center in Houston, Texas, as a National Research Council Resident Research Associate. For this position, scholars apply to certain government agencies to do high-level research of their choosing. It is a very difficult program to get into.

She also applied for the astronaut program over and over, but was always turned down. In ten years, she applied ten times! Finally, in 1992, she was put in charge of a joint science mission between the United States and Russia. She was in the right place at the right time. A mission was coming up called the NASA/MIR, Shuttle/MIR Project.

When it came to space exploration, Russia and the United States had a long history of competing with each other. In 1975, there was a test project called the Apollo/Soyuz. It was the first collaborative effort between the two countries. Years later, this cooperation made the NASA/MIR program possible. The purpose of the MIR Shuttle Program was to create a laboratory in space—the Mir Space Station. There, multiple countries could work together, performing scientific experiments in space.

Dr. Shannon Lucid, astronaut and cosmonaut guest researcher, works out on a treadmill device aboard the Base Block Module on Russia's Mir Space Station.

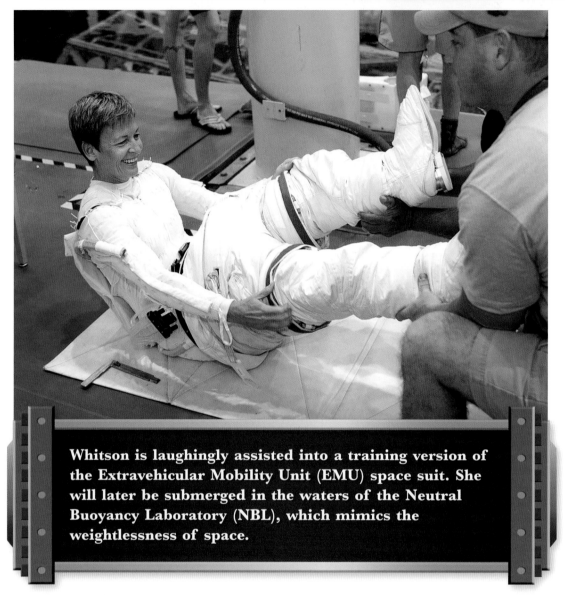

Whitson is laughingly assisted into a training version of the Extravehicular Mobility Unit (EMU) space suit. She will later be submerged in the waters of the Neutral Buoyancy Laboratory (NBL), which mimics the weightlessness of space.

Since Whitson had been organizing the project on the ground, it made sense for her to continue overseeing the NASA/MIR Project in space. "It wasn't until I was on the selection board that I realized how lucky I was," Whitson told *USA Today*. "We had 8,400 [astronaut applicants], and we picked eight."[6]

Now there weren't any more barriers between Whitson and her dream of being an astronaut. It was time for training!

Clarence Sams

Clarence Sams grew up fascinated by both flying planes and space travel. In 1984, he joined NASA and got the best of both worlds.

Sams became the director of the Cell and Molecular Research Laboratory in Houston, Texas. There, he ran tests on how space travel affects the human body at the cellular level, as well as the effects on the immune system. Sams was the project scientist for the Countermeasure Evaluation and Validation Project. He also served as a research adviser in the National Research Council Resident Research Associateship Program. Sams also found the time to teach classes at Rice University and at Texas Houston Medical School.

As Sams said in his NASA bio, "Most pilots fly because they love to fly. The good ones are always learning." Throughout his NASA career and his life, Sams has been best known for his ability to learn new things, change directions, and meet challenges with excitement.[7]

Sams met Peggy Whitson when both were studying for their doctorates in chemistry at Rice University in the 1980s.

NASA chose this KC-135 as the perfect aircraft for its Reduced Gravity Program. It alternates steep climbs and dives to produce weightlessness for its passengers. The aircraft earned the nickname of UC Vomit Comet for obvious reasons.

Her First
Mission to Space

In 1996, Whitson began astronaut training. This training can take up to two years to complete. It tests a person's body and mind. For their bodies, trainees swim underwater, wear large and heavy suits while trying to move large and heavy objects, and take rides in the infamous Vomit Comet. To train their minds, they take classes in many science-based subjects, wilderness survival, and public speaking. Trainees also take courses in biology, physics, and astrophysics. They become familiar with electrical engineering and computer programing, too. This way, if a problem arises in space, astronauts can find solutions on their own.

Whitson graduated from astronaut training in 1998. She continued to work closely with Russia on the joint space station project until, in 2002, the only work left to do was in space.

Whitson's first trip to the stars came on June 5, 2002, when she flew with the Expedition 5 team to the International Space Station (ISS). Two days later, the shuttle *Endeavour* docked with the ISS. The *Endeavour* stayed docked for eight days. During this time, the crew

Peggy Whitson (center) partners with Russian cosmonauts Valery G. Korzun (left) and Sergei Y. Treshchev to form the crew of Expedition 5, the fifth long-duration stay in space. They remained in space for 184 days, 178 of them aboard the ISS.

already aboard the ISS helped orient the newly arrived crew. After eight days, the previous ISS crew boarded *Endeavour* and took it back to Earth.[1]

Expedition 5 accomplished a lot during the team's time in space. They ran tests on what happened to the human body during space travel. From one end of the ISS to the other, they tested all of the robotics on board. Two spacewalks (Extra Vehicular Activity or EVA) were taken, but Whitson got to take the first! The goal of the EVA was to install six debris panels on the outside of the ISS. These panels would protect the ISS from free-floating space debris.[2]

Peggy Whitson was the mission's science officer. This was a new role created by NASA administrator Sean O'Keefe, and Whitson was the first person to hold the position. The science officer's job was to oversee all U.S. experiments and research aboard the ISS. More than that, she was also responsible for continuing the experiments and research once she returned to the ground.

Peggy Whitson works aboard the ISS during one of her 665 days in space.

Whitson described one of her first spacewalks to *Business Insider*. On the outside of the ISS, she had been working with a set of solar panels. "I could see myself in a space suit, I could see the Earth behind me in the solar arrays, and I was like, 'Holy cow, I really am an astronaut!' Because you forget."[3]

There was trouble during Whitson's first time in space. On September 21, 2002, Hurricane Lili was predicted to come very close to Houston's Mission Control Center (MCCH). In one of the letters Whitson wrote to the public back on Earth, she described what Hurricane Lili looked like from above. "From our vantage point, the eye of the hurricane really did look like an eye, with a well-defined shape and edges. Lili's skirt was formed by the surrounding clouds, which appeared to be sucked into a swirling dance around the eye."[4] As beautiful as it was from space, on the ground, Lili spelled catastrophe.

To prepare for the storm, MCCH shut down all communications with the ISS. During this time, many of the systems aboard the ISS had to be shut down as well. The power on the ISS was closely linked to the power at the MCCH. If the ISS detected that the MCCH was low on power, which could happen during the hurricane, the ISS could start

The swirling eye of Hurricane Lili over the Gulf of Mexico on October 2, 2002. Lili's deadly winds and rains on the ground also posed a threat to those on the ISS.

powering down sections of the station all by itself. To keep this from happening, Whitson and her crew chose which sections to shut down themselves.[5]

Fortunately, Hurricane Lili missed MCCH. After two days of radio silence, communications resumed, and life as usual continued aboard the ISS.

On November 25, the *Endeavour* returned to the ISS with a few more crew members to join Whitson's. The new crew members had brought different food, an exciting event. They also brought Whitson a gift from her husband: a pecan pie!

A few days later, Whitson and her crewmates boarded the shuttle and returned to Earth, arriving on December 7, 2002. Her first mission to space had lasted 184 days. She had spent 22 hours in EVAs, and she felt deeply changed by it. "To be a participant in all of this is unbelievable, even to me as I float here and write this, knowing you can see a speck of light speeding by in the early morning sky or at dusk, and knowing that I am in that bit of light."[6]

Eating in Space

Eating food in space can be complicated. In the early days of spaceflight, food came out of tubes or in the form of dried cubes. While options have improved, there are still problems. The ISS, for instance, does not have a refrigerator. Fruits and vegetables go bad even more quickly in space than they do on the ground. Most types must be eaten within seven days of leaving Earth. Carrots and celery sticks have to be eaten within two days!

The difficulty of eating aboard the ISS doesn't end with fresh food, either. Liquid forms of salt and pepper have to be used. If the regular kinds were used, the bits of salt and pepper would shoot off into the air. There would even be the risk of them getting caught in air vents, messing with equipment, or getting stuck in an astronaut's eyes or nose.[7]

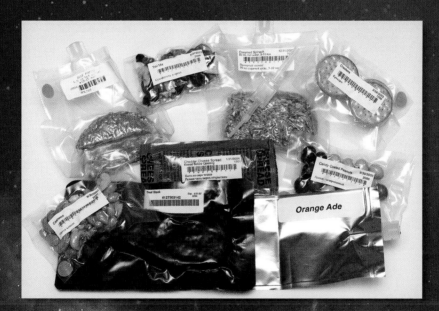

NASA space food scientists are continually working to provide future crews traveling to the moon and Mars with safe, nutritious, and appetizing food.

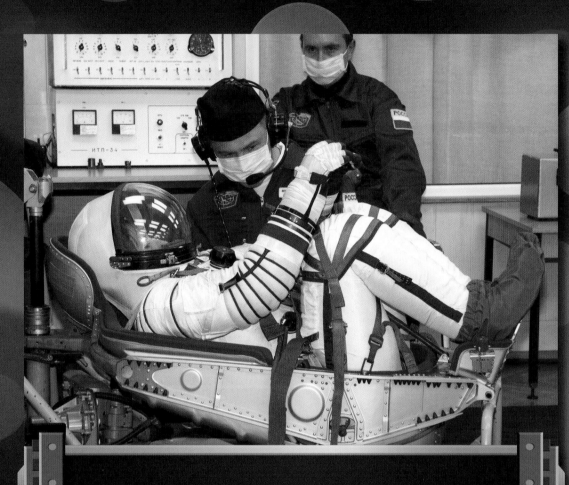

Whitson suits up in a pressurized Sokol spacesuit in preparation for Expedition 16, the 16th expedition to the ISS.

CHAPTER 4

Breaking Records

Once Peggy Whitson had her first taste of being in space, she wanted more. She returned from her first trip at the end of 2002, and wouldn't make her next visit to the stars until 2008. During the years between, Whitson filled a few different roles at NASA. She was the Chief of the Station Operations Branch Astronaut Office. She was trained as the backup ISS commander for Expedition 14, but in the end she wasn't needed. Whitson was made a member of the Astronaut Selection Board in 2004, giving her influence over who was chosen for the astronaut program.

On October 10, 2007, Whitson went back to the ISS as a member of Expedition 16. This time, she was the mission commander. She described her new role to *Business Insider*: "You're responsible for crew safety, and the safety of the vehicle, so, you know, it ups the stress level a bit."[1] Whitson oversaw the expansion of the parts of the ISS the crew used for relaxation. This included the living and working spaces. It was the first time these areas had seen expansion in six years!

Expedition 16 crew bonds with *Endeavour* astronauts prior to departing the ISS on March 24, 2008. On this expedition, Peggy Whitson (center) became the first female commander of an ISS mission.

Whitson also performed five spacewalks during these six months in space.

Whitson told *Space.com*, "On my first flight, I don't know if maybe it's a function of time, or if I was less stressed on my second flight, but just being able to tell what part of the planet we were flying over by the reflected light coming through the window—that was pretty special. To be able to say, 'Oh, we're flying over northern Africa now,' because of the warm peachy glow of the light coming through, that was really special . . . and [I could] take a little bit more time to just be in awe of it all."[2]

After 192 days in space, Whitson returned to Earth on April 19, 2008. It would be another eight years before she returned to the ISS.

Whitson spent that time in the largest, most important role of her career so far. She was Chief of the Astronaut Corps, where she was responsible for the preparations for shuttle launches. Whitson was also in charge of supporting crews aboard the ISS. This was the first time NASA had ever hired a female as Chief of the Astronaut Corps.

Whitson's third launch came in 2016 as a member of Expedition 50. At nine and a half months, it would be her longest trip yet. NASA received 18,000 applications for just 12 positions. Whitson went back

During her seventh spacewalk on Expedition 50 in 2017, Whitson hooks up new lithium-ion batteries and inspects the Alpha Magnetic Spectrometer.

Celebrating the holidays in space on Expedition 50, Whitson sends greetings from the cupola of the ISS on December 24, 2016.

to the ISS as one of those 12, once again as the station commander. Not only was she the only female to have held the role, but she was also the only woman to hold the position twice. This wasn't the only record she broke. She was 56 years old on her third voyage to the stars, making her the oldest female astronaut to visit space.

Space travel is hard on the human body. It would be even harder on Whitson's because of her age. To make sure she was ready, she underwent an additional 19 hours of astronaut training and medical testing. "We go everywhere on that space station with our hands," Whitson told *Business Insider*. "Everything's very hand intensive, so your hands do have a tendency to get very tired." Aboard the ISS, astronauts work out two hours every day to keep their bodies in shape.[3]

Whitson participated in four spacewalks on her third stay aboard the ISS. This brought her total to 10, the most spacewalks ever undertaken by a female astronaut. She had spent a total of 60 hours and 21 minutes outside in space. Only three other people in the world had been on spacewalks that totaled more time than hers.

Crew members Peggy Whitson, Thomas Pesquet, and Oleg Novitsky train for expeditions 50 and 51 on September 17, 2015.

European Space Agency astronaut Samantha Cristoforetti photographed this spectacular image of Earth—clearly the Blue Planet—from the ISS on December 9, 2014.

On September 3, 2017, Whitson returned to Earth for the last time. A year later, she retired from NASA, but she had a lot to show for it. She'd broken so many records, people were talking about her all over the world in newspapers, magazines, and books. She told the Associated Press how she would miss seeing Earth from above: "Until the end of my days, my eyes will search the horizon to see that curve."[4]

The Life of the ISS

Construction of the International Space Station began in 1998 and, in many ways, has continued ever since. Parts of the station are constantly being added, changed, and improved. When it was originally constructed, it was through the combined effort of 16 nations. The ISS was built by bringing all its different parts into space and putting them together. The modules are the areas with breathable air, such as the laboratories, equipment rooms, and living spaces. For example, Destiny is the module that houses the U.S. lab; Columbus houses the European lab; and Kibo houses the Japanese lab. Nodes were originally designed just to connect the modules, but some of them, such as Node-3, are as complex as the modules. Node-3 is also called Tranquility. It holds exercise equipment, showers, and systems that control airflow and air temperature. It also provides additional docking ports for the space station.

The ISS is scheduled to be retired in 2024. Some parts of the station will stay in space and be incorporated into Russia's new station, the Orbital Piloted Assembly and Experiment Complex (OPSEK). One of these will be the module Zarya, which also happens to have been the first module sent into space when the ISS was built.[5]

Whitson conducts an experiment on pressure in the Destiny laboratory of the ISS.

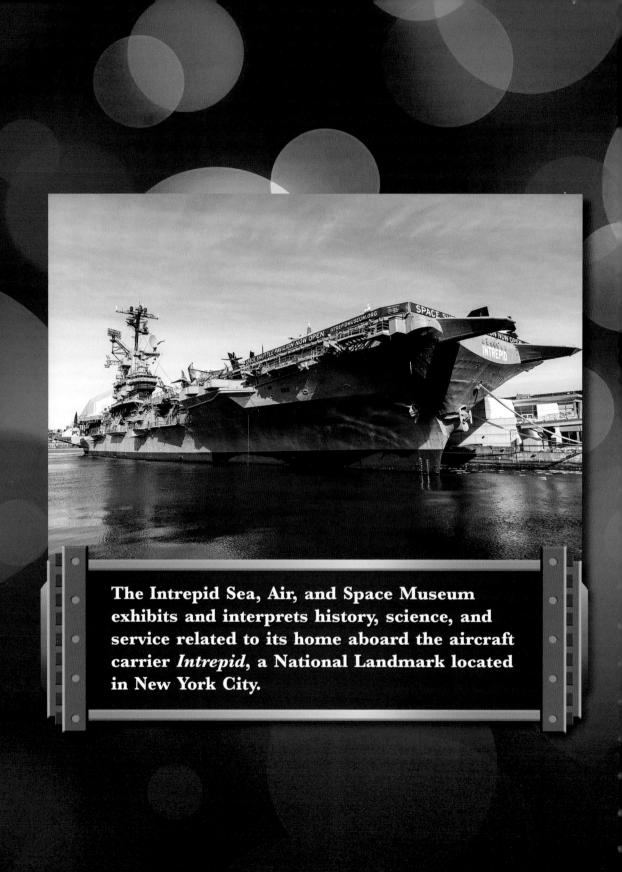

The Intrepid Sea, Air, and Space Museum exhibits and interprets history, science, and service related to its home aboard the aircraft carrier *Intrepid*, a National Landmark located in New York City.

CHAPTER 5

Bringing Space Down to Earth

Peggy Whitson has received worldwide recognition throughout her NASA career and after her retirement in 2018. In 2006, she was awarded the NASA Outstanding Leadership Medal. In 2011, she was added to the Iowa Aviation Hall of Fame, and she was named one of Houston's 50 Most Influential Women. In 2018, *Time* named her one of its 100 Most Influential People.

Even after Whitson returned to the ground, she did not stop trying to share her love for space with the world, and especially with children. In February 2018, she participated in Kids Week at the Intrepid Sea, Air and Space Museum. The program was called "So You Want to Go to Mars?" Whitson handed out samples of the food astronauts ate in space.[1] She told *Space.com*, "The floating, the sleeping, just being in zero gravity—it's so much easier to move. My joints don't ache near as much up there. I love being in space."[2]

In March 2018, Whitson appeared on the cover of *National Geographic*. In some ways, this was to get people excited about a new TV series National Geographic would be launching, called *One Strange*

Bon appétit! **Flight Engineers Sergei Treshchev and Peggy Whitson dine space-style amid floating tomatoes and other select space-worthy cuisine aboard the ISS.**

Rock. Hosted by actor Will Smith, the ten-episode documentary was about life on Earth, but it was told in the voices of people who had looked down on Earth from space. Eight astronauts, including Whitson, participated. The final episode was called "There's No Place Like Home" and focused on a typical day in Whitson's life board the ISS. This included everything from performing scientific experiments to staring out the window at Earth or just brushing her teeth.[3]

When astronauts return to Earth, most of them feel a strong desire to share their experience with others. For most of them, it is impossible to find the right words. This change in how they see the planet is so common in astronauts, it has come to be called the "overview effect." In an interview with *Space.com*, Whitson said, "I came away from my first flight with this new appreciation of how we're all sharing the same air, we're all sharing the same planet, and we need to take care of it."[4]

When Whitson retired from NASA on June 15, 2018, NASA Administrator Jim Bridenstine was sad to see her go. "Peggy Whitson is a testament to the American spirit," he told *Space.com*. "Her

Former U.S. Navy pilot and U.S. Representative from Oklahoma James Frederick "Jim" Bridenstine was sworn in as NASA's thirteenth administrator on April 23, 2018.

Retired NASA astronaut Pat Forrester (right), who has been working with SpaceX, watches the launch of the Dragon spacecraft and crew into orbit with Chief Flight Director Norm Knight (center) and astronaut Bob Behnken.

determination, strength of mind, character, and dedication to science, exploration, and discovery are an inspiration to NASA and America."[5]

Bridenstine wasn't the only person at NASA to be saddened by Whitson's retirement. "Peggy is a classmate and a friend, and she will be deeply missed," Pat Forrester, the chief of the Astronaut Office, told *Space.com*. "Along with her record-setting career, she leaves behind a legacy of her passion for space."[6]

People were proud of Peggy Whitson, but few places were as proud as where she was born: Ayr, Iowa. Ken Robertson came up with the idea of creating a Peggy Whitson Rock. Robertson called Whitson to see what she thought. "She like[d] the idea," Robertson told *KMALand*. "All she asked was that it have an American flag."[7]

In early December, the Peggy Whitson Rock was finished. It weighed 60,000 pounds and had a plate saying, "Peggy A. Whitson. Born 2/9/60 – Mt. Ayr, Iowa. Hometown – Beaconsfield, Iowa. 10 space walks. 665 days in space."[8] True to Whitson's request, Robertson made sure an American flag was painted over the top of the rock. Mount Ayr community members unveiled the Peggy Whitson Freedom Rock on Saturday afternoon, April 6, 2019. When *KMALand* asked Robertson about the project, he said, "She comes to town, and she comes and talks to the school, and everybody in the school just gets excited. . . . I think it helps the kids understand that you can accomplish anything you want to in this world."[9]

Peggy Whitson might be finished traveling to the stars, but that doesn't stop her from encouraging others to make the trip. In fact, if she has spent her time since leaving NASA doing anything, it has been telling the world to dream big. When asked in an interview with *Space Station Explorers* what she'd say to the youth of today, Whitson said, "One is to find your passion. . . . You need to love what you're doing. Your journey in life has to be fun for you. And then work to make it happen. Don't expect somebody to hand you the perfect job just because you dreamed about it. . . . I think you can find out you're capable of so much more than what you might even dream of."[10]

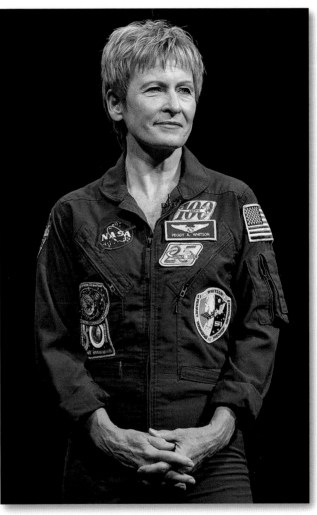

Whitson stands at ease during an interview at Smithsonian's Air and Space Museum in Washington, D.C.

Peggy Whitson had started out as a girl on a farm staring up at the stars. She reached those stars through her planning, her drive, and her perseverance. With that combination, a kid could be anything he or she wants.

Women In Space

As of March 2019, over 60 women have left Earth to explore space. One of the most recent was Christina Koch, who who would be on the ISS for Expedition 59, 60, and 61, for a total of 328 days.

Anne McClain, a flight engineer, made her journey to study the negative effects of microgravity. She is an Army Aviator, logging more than 2,000 flight hours.

Serena Auñón-Chancellor found her way to space to research Angiex Cancer Therapy. She also is helping people understand how such work in space might produce cost-effective and safer treatments.

1960   Peggy Annette Whitson is born on February 9 in Mount Ayr, Iowa.

1969   She enrolls at the Mount Ayr Community High School.

1978   She graduates from high school and enrolls at Iowa Wesleyan College.

1979   Whitson is declared a State of Iowa Scholar.

1980   She receives the Orange van Calhoun Scholarship.

1981   Whitson graduates with a bachelor's degree in science.

1989   She marries fellow NASA employee Clarence Sams.

1996   Whitson begins astronaut training.

1998   She graduates from astronaut training. Construction of the International Space Station begins.

2002   Whitson makes her first trip to the ISS as part of Expedition 5.

2004   She is made a member of the Astronaut Selection Board.

2006   She receives the NASA Outstanding Leadership Medal.

2007   Whitson flies back to the ISS with Expedition 16 as the mission commander.

2008   At NASA, she is made the first female Chief of the Astronaut Corps.

2011   She is added to the Iowa Aviation Hall of Fame.

2016   Whitson flies back to the ISS with Expedition 50.

2018   Whitson retires from NASA. She is featured on the cover of *National Geographic* and on National Geographic's documentary series *One Strange Rock*.

2019   The Peggy Whitson Rock is unveiled in Ayr, Iowa.

2024   The ISS is scheduled to be retired.

Peggy Whitson climbs the ropes of Maxwell's Officer Training School with ease on May 23, 2013.

CHAPTER NOTES

Chapter One: Ignore the Naysayers

1. "Note to Self: From space, Astronaut Peggy Whitson Tells Her Younger Self: 'Ignore the Naysayers.' " *CBS News*, January 21, 2018. https://www.cbsnews.com/news/astronaut-peggy-whitson-note-to-self/
2. Ibid.
3. Ibid.
4. Ibid.
5. Ibid.
6. Ibid.
7. Ibid.
8. Ibid.

Chapter Two: The Farm Girl Goes to NASA

1. "Preflight Interviews: Peggy Whitson." *NASA*. September 28, 2007. https://www.nasa.gov/mission_pages/station/expeditions/expedition16/exp16_interview_whitson.html
2. "Peggy Whitson: First Female Commander of the International Space Station." *Makers.com*, n.d. https://www.makers.com/videos/599349aa83b51f47e161750a
3. "Preflight Interviews: Peggy Whitson."
4. Mike Kilen, "Age Is No Barrier for Astronaut Peggy Whitson." *USA Today*, March 17, 2015. https://www.usatoday.com/story/news/nation/2015/03/17/age-barrier-astronaut-peggy-whitson/24941597/
5. Ibid.
6. Ibid.
7. "Profiles: Clarence Sams Biochemist." NASA Education, February 5, 2004. https://www.nasa.gov/audience/foreducators/postsecondary/features/F_Clarence_Sams_Biochemist.html

Chapter Three: Her First Mission to Space

1. "Peggy A. Whitson (Ph.D.), NASA Astronaut." NASA, December 24, 2018. https://www.nasa.gov/astronauts/biographies/peggy-a-whitson/biography
2. Ibid.
3. Hilary Brueck, "The Incredible Career of NASA's Peggy Whitson, Who Applied to Become an Astronaut 10 Times Before She Broke the American Record for Space Travel." *Business Insider*, June 15, 2018. https://www.businessinsider.com/nasa-astronaut-peggy-whitson-career-2018-6
4. "Expedition Five: Letters Home #12." *NASA, Space Flight*. Unknown date. https://spaceflight.nasa.gov/station/crew/exp5/lettershome12.html
5. Ibid.

6. "Expedition Five: Letters Home #13." *NASA, Space Flight*. Unknown date. https://spaceflight.nasa. gov/station/crew/exp5/lettershome.html

7. "Eating in Space." *NASA*, June 27, 2018. https://www.nasa.gov/audience/foreducators/stem-on-station/ditl_eating

Chapter Four: Breaking Records

1. Hilary Brueck, "The Incredible Career of NASA's Peggy Whitson, Who Applied to Become an Astronaut 10 Times Before She Broke the American Record for Space Travel." *Business Insider*, June 15, 2018. https://www.businessinsider.com/nasa-astronaut-peggy-whitson-career-2018-6

2. Clara Moskowitz, "Life on a Space Station: Q&A with NASA's Chief Astronaut Peggy Whitson." *Space.com*, November 12, 2010. https://www.space.com/90-life-space-station-nasa-chief-astronaut-peggy-whitson.html

3. Brueck.

4. "Peggy Whitson, NASA's Record-Breaking Spacewoman, Retires as Astronaut." *Associated Press*, June 16, 2018. https://www.nbcnews.com/mach/news/ peggy-whitson-nasa-s-record-breaking-spacewoman-retires-astronaut-ncna883906

5. "International Space Station Facts and Figures." *NASA*. November 5, 2018. https://www.nasa.gov/ feature/facts-and-figures

Chapter Five: Bringing Space Down to Earth

1. Doris Elin Salazar, "'So You Want to Go to Mars': Astronaut Peggy Whitson and Scientists Inspire NYC Kids." *Space.com*, March 5, 2018. https://www.space.com/39860-astronaut-peggy-whitson-inspires-nyc-kids.html

2. Hanneke Weitering, "Astronaut Peggy Whitson Comes 'Home' in 'One Strange Rock Finale.'" *Space. com*, May 28, 2018. https://www.space.com/40719-one-strange-rock-finale-peggy-whitson.html

3. Ibid.

4. Ibid.

5. Mike Wall, "Record-Breaking Astronaut Peggy Whitson Retires from NASA." *Space.com*, June 15, 2018. https://www.space.com/40909-record-breaking-nasa-astronaut-peggy-whitson-retires.html

6. Ibid.

7. Mike Peterson, "Whitson Rock Honors Ringgold County Native." *KMALand*, December 27, 2018. http://www.kmaland.com/news/whitson-rock-honors-ringgold-county-native/article_b619717a-09eb-11e9-9584-3b766902dd2d.html

8. Ibid.

9. Ibid.

10. "Let Record-Breaking Astronaut Peggy Whitson Inspire You." *Space Station Explorers*, July 16, 2018. https://www.spacestationexplorers.org/let-record-breaking-astronaut-peggy-whitson-inspire-you/

Books

Gregory, Josh. *If You Were a Kid Docking at the International Space Station*. New York: Children's Press, 2017.

Jackson, Libby. *Galaxy Girls: 50 Amazing Stories of Women in Space*. New York: Harper Design, 2018.

King, Gayle. *Note to Self: Inspiring Words from Inspiring People*. New York: Simon and Schuster, 2018.

National Geographic. *Through an Astronaut's Eyes*. Washington, D.C.: National Geographic 2018.

O'Shaughnessy, Tam. *Sally Ride: A Photobiography of America's Pioneering Woman in Space*. New York: Roaring Brook Press, 2015.

Richmond, Ben. *Life in Space*. New York: Sterling Children's Books, 2018.

Works Consulted

Associated Press. "Peggy Whitson, NASA's Record-Breaking Spacewoman, Retires as Astronaut." *Associated Press*, June 16, 2018. https://www.nbcnews.com/mach/news/peggy-whitson-nasa-s-record-breaking-spacewoman-retires-astronaut-ncna883906

Brueck, Hilary. "The Incredible Career of NASA's Peggy Whitson, Who Applied to Become an Astronaut 10 Times Before She Broke the American Record for Space Travel." *Business Insider*, June 15, 2018. https://www.businessinsider.com/nasa-astronaut-peggy-whitson-career-2018-6

CBS News: "From Space, Astronaut Peggy Whitson Tells Her Younger Self: 'Ignore the Naysayers.'" *CBS News*. November 10, 2017. https://www.cbsnews.com/news/astronaut-peggy-whitson-note-to-self/

CBS News. "Note to Self." *CBS News*. Unknown date. https://www.cbsnews.com/cbs-this-morning/note-to-self/

Dooley, Erin. "U.S. Astronaut Peggy Whitson Breaks American Space Flight Record." *ABC News*, April 24, 2017. https://abcnews.go.com/US/us-astronaut-peggy-whitson-breaks-american-spaceflight-record/story?id=46976358

Giorgio Mills, Katie. "NASA Astronaut Peggy Whitson's 5 Tips for Success." *The Week*, March 5, 2018. https://theweek.com/articles/751866/nasa-astronaut-peggy-whitsons-5-tips-success

Kilen, Mike. "Age Is No Barrier for Astronaut Peggy Whitson." *USA Today*, March 17, 2015. https://www.usatoday.com/story/news/nation/2015/03/17/age-barrier-astronaut-peggy-whitson/24941597/

King, Alexandra. "Peggy Whitson has Spent More Time in Space than Any Other American. This Is What It's Like." *CNN*, May 1, 2017. https://www.cnn.com/2017/05/01/us/peggy-whitson-fb-live-interview-trnd-cnntv/index.html

Lewis, Ben. "Astronaut Peggy Whitson Calls It a Day." *Australia Science*, July 5, 2018. https://australiascience.tv/space-pic-of-the-week-farewell-peggy-whitson/

Makers.com. "Peggy Whitson: First Female Commander of the International Space Station." *Makers.com*, n.d. https://www.makers.com/videos/599349aa83b51f47e161750a

Moskowitz, Clara. "Life On a Space Station: Q&A with NASA's Chief Astronaut Peggy Whitson." *Space.com*, November 12, 2010. https://www.space.com/90-life-space-station-nasa-chief-astronaut-peggy-whitson.html

NASA. "International Space Station Facts and Figures." *NASA*. November 5, 2018. https://www.nasa.gov/feature/facts-and-figures

NASA. "Eating in Space." *NASA*, June 27, 2018. https://www.nasa.gov/audience/foreducators/stem-on-station/ditl_eating

NASA. "Expedition Five: Letters Home #12." *NASA*: Space Flight. Unknown date. https://spaceflight.nasa.gov/station/crew/exp5/lettershome12.html

NASA. "Expedition Five: Letters Home #13." *NASA*: Space Flight. Unknown date. https://spaceflight.nasa.gov/station/crew/exp5/lettershome.html

NASA. "NASA Astronaut Peggy Whitson Shares Thoughts on Extended Mission, Returning to Earth." *NASA*, September 1, 2017. https://www.nasa.gov/feature/nasa-astronaut-peggy-whitson-shares-thoughts-on-extended-mission-returning-to-earth

NASA. "Peggy A. Whitson, NASA Astronaut." *NASA*, n.d. https://www.nasa.gov/astronauts/biographies/peggy-a-whitson/biography

NASA. "Preflight Interviews: Peggy Whitson." *NASA*, September 28, 2007. https://www.nasa.gov/mission_pages/station/expeditions/expedition16/exp16_interview_whitson.html

NASA. "Profiles: Clarence Sams Biochemist." *NASA*, February 5, 2004. https://www.nasa.gov/audience/foreducators/postsecondary/features/F_Clarence_Sams_Biochemist.html

NASA. "Space Station Assembly." November 20, 2018. https://www.nasa.gov/mission_pages/station/structure/elements/space-station-assembly

Pesquet, Thomas. "Peggy Whitson." *Time 100*, 2018. http://time.com/collection/most-influential-people-2018/5217644/peggy-whitson/

Peterson, Mike. "Whitson Rock Honors Ringgold County Native." *KMALand*, December 27, 2018. http://www.kmaland.com/news/whitson-rock-honors-ringgold-county-native/article_b619717a-09eb-11e9-9584-3b766902dd2d.html

Salazar, Doris Elin. "'So You Want to Go to Mars:' Astronaut Peggy Whitson and Scientists Inspire NYC Kids." *Space.com*, March 5, 2018. https://www.space.com/39860-astronaut-peggy-whitson-inspires-nyc-kids.html

Space Station Explorers. "Let Record-Breaking Astronaut Peggy Whitson Inspire You." *Space Station Explorers*, July 16, 2018. https://www.spacestationexplorers.org/let-record-breaking-astronaut-peggy-whitson-inspire-you/

Wall, Mike. "Record-Breaking Astronaut Peggy Whitson Retires from NASA." *Space.com*, June 15, 2018. https://www.space.com/40909-record-breaking-nasa-astronaut-peggy-whitson-retires.html

Weitering, Hanneke. "Astronaut Peggy Whitson Comes 'Home' in 'One Strange Rock Finale.'" *Space.com*, May 28, 2018. https://www.space.com/40719-one-strange-rock-finale-peggy-whitson.html

On the Internet

"Female Astronaut Sets Super Space Records." *National Geographic Kids*, unknown date. https://www.natgeokids.com/au/discover/science/space/astronaut-peggy-whitson-record-breaking/

NASA: "International Space Station." https://www.nasa.gov/mission_pages/station/main/index.html

NASA: "NASA Astronaut Peggy A. Whitson." https://www.nasa.gov/astronauts/biographies/peggy-a-whitson

National Geographic: "Peggy Whitson Bio." https://www.nationalgeographic.com.au/people/peggy-whitson-bio.aspx

astrophysics (AS-troh-fih-ziks)—The scientific study of the stars.

biochemistry (BY-oh-KEH-mih-stree)—The study of living organisms.

dock—To connect two vehicles in space.

docking port—The area of a space vehicle where another space vehicle can connect.

encompass (en-KOM-pus)—To totally enclose or surround.

module (MOD-jyool)—The parts of the ISS with breathable air, such as the living quarters.

naysayer (NAY-say-er)—A person who always says "no" to new ideas.

node (NOHD)—One of the parts of the International Space Station that connect the modules.

orbit (OR-bit)—The path of an object around a moon or planet.

physicist (FIH-zih-sist)—A scientist who studies motion and forces.

radio silence (RAY-dee-oh SY-lents)—The shutdown of all communications.

reputation (reh-pyoo-TAY-shun)—The qualities a person is known for.

solar array (SOH-lur ah-RAY)—A group of panels designed to change sunlight into electrical power.

testament (TES-tuh-munt)—Something that serves as proof or evidence.

unveil (un-VAYL)—To uncover or reveal.

Vomit Comet (VAH-mit KAH-mit)—The machine NASA uses to train astronauts in zero gravity.

The CST-100 Starliner, Boeing's space capsule for the 21st century, is designed to carry seven passengers—or a mix of crew and cargo—into low-Earth orbit.

PHOTO CREDITS: Cover, p 1—NASA, Public Domain; pp. 4, 6, 7, 9, 12, 16, 16, 17, 18, 21, 22, 23, 24, 25, 26, 27, 31, 34, 36, 38, 39, 47—NASA; p. 8—USDA; p. 10—Pixabay; pp. 13, 14, 20—Public Domain; p. 29—James Blair/NASA; p. 30—Samantha Cristoforetti/NASA; p. 32—Joao Carlos Medau; pp. 35, 37—Joel Kowsky/ NASA; p. 44—Donna Burnett. Every measure has been taken to find all copyright holders of material used in this book. In the event any mistakes or omissions have happened within, attempts to correct them will be made in future editions of the book.